Praise for *Insid*

"What C-level executives read to keep th
decisions. Timeless classics for indispensa
Manager of Corporate Marketing Commun

"Want to know what the real leaders are thinking about now? It's in here." - Carl Ledbetter, SVP and CTO, Novell, Inc.

"Priceless wisdom from experts at applying technology in support of business objectives." - Frank Campagnoni, CTO, GE Global Exchange Services

"Unique insights into the way the experts think and the lessons they've learned from experience." - MT Rainey, Co-CEO, Young & Rubicam/Rainey Kelly Campbell Roalfe

"A must-read for anyone in the industry." - Dr. Chuck Lucier, Chief Growth Officer, Booz-Allen & Hamilton

"Unlike any other business books, *Inside the Minds* captures the essence, the deep-down thinking processes, of people who make things happen." - Martin Cooper, CEO, Arraycomm

"A must-read for those who manage at the intersection of business and technology." - Frank Roney, General Manager, IBM

"A great way to see across the changing marketing landscape at a time of significant innovation." - David Kenny, Chairman and CEO, Digitas

"An incredible resource of information to help you develop outside the box..." - Rich Jernstedt, CEO, Golin/Harris International

"A snapshot of everything you need to know..." - Larry Weber, Founder, Weber Shandwick

"Great information for both novices and experts." - Patrick Ennis, Partner, ARCH Venture Partners

"The only useful way to get so many good minds speaking on a complex topic." - Scott Bradner, Senior Technical Consultant, Harvard University

"Must-have information for business executives." - Alex Wilmerding, Principal, Boston Capital Ventures

www.Aspatore.com

Aspatore Books is the largest and most exclusive publisher of C-level executives (CEO, CFO, CTO, CMO, partner) from the world's most respected companies. Aspatore annually publishes C-level executives from over half the Global 500, top 250 professional services firms, law firms (MPs/chairs), and other leading companies of all sizes. By focusing on publishing only C-level executives, Aspatore provides professionals of all levels with proven business intelligence from industry insiders, rather than relying on the knowledge of unknown authors and analysts. Aspatore Books is committed to publishing a highly innovative line of business books, redefining and expanding the meaning of such books as indispensable resources for professionals of all levels. In addition to individual best-selling business titles, Aspatore Books publishes the following unique lines of business books: Inside the Minds, Business Bibles, Bigwig Briefs, C-Level Business Review (Quarterly), Book Binders, ExecRecs, and The C-Level Test, innovative resources for all professionals. Aspatore is a privately held company headquartered in Boston, Massachusetts, with employees around the world.

Inside the Minds

The critically acclaimed *Inside the Minds* series provides readers of all levels with proven business intelligence from C-level executives (CEO, CFO, CTO, CMO, partner) from the world's most respected companies. Each chapter is comparable to a white paper or essay and is a future-oriented look at where an industry/profession/topic is heading and the most important issues for future success. Each author has been carefully chosen through an exhaustive selection process by the *Inside the Minds* editorial board to write a chapter for this book. *Inside the Minds* was conceived in order to give readers actual insights into the leading minds of business executives worldwide. Because so few books or other publications are actually written by executives in industry, *Inside the Minds* presents an unprecedented look at various industries and professions never before available.

INSIDE THE MINDS

Consumer Products and Services

Leadership Strategies of Top CEOs

BOOK IDEA SUBMISSIONS

If you are a C-level executive or senior lawyer interested in submitting a book idea or manuscript to the Aspatore editorial board, please e-mail authors@aspatore.com. Aspatore is especially looking for highly specific book ideas that would have a direct financial impact on behalf of a reader. Completed books can range from 20 to 2,000 pages–the topic and "need to read" aspect of the material are most important, not the length. Include your book idea, biography, and any additional pertinent information.

SPEAKER SUBMISSIONS FOR CONFERENCES

If you are interested in giving a speech for an upcoming ReedLogic conference (a partner of Aspatore Books), please e-mail the ReedLogic Speaker Board at speakers@reedlogic.com. If selected, speeches are given over the phone and recorded (no travel necessary). Due to the busy schedules and travel implications for executives, ReedLogic produces each conference on CD-ROM, then distributes the conference to bookstores and executives who register for the conference. The finished CD-ROM includes the speaker picture with the audio of the speech playing in the background, similar to a radio address played on television.

INTERACTIVE SOFTWARE SUBMISSIONS

If you have an idea for an interactive business or software legal program, please e-mail software@reedlogic.com. ReedLogic is especially looking for Excel spreadsheet models and PowerPoint presentations that help business professionals and lawyers achieve specific tasks. If idea or program is accepted, product is distributed to bookstores nationwide.

Published by Aspatore, Inc.
For corrections, company/title updates, comments, or any other inquiries, please e-mail store@aspatore.com.

First Printing, 2005
10 9 8 7 6 5 4 3 2 1

ISBN 1-59622-140-2
Library of Congress Control Number: 2005933687

Inside the Minds Managing Editor, Leah M. Jones, Edited by Laura Knox, Proofread by Eddie Fournier

Consumer Products and Services

Leading Strategies of Top CEOs

CONTENTS

Creating Successful Products that Deliver Profits

Andrew R. Gatto

President and Chief Executive Officer

Russ Berrie and Company Inc.

Achieving Success in the Consumer Products Industry

To succeed, companies must win consumer loyalty by providing exceptional value through their brands. Today's consumer is far more demanding in terms of the value proposition he or she is being served with. That value doesn't necessarily need to come in the form of cheap prices; it has more to do with price value. In the consumer products industry, people expect a certain level of quality and post-purchase satisfaction for whatever amount of money they invest in a product. Companies don't want to miss meeting consumers' expectations; it's to their advantage to exceed expectations.

Business Approach and Generating Revenue

This company has been in existence for more than forty years, and it has strongly committed itself to a level of quality that has been uncompromised. The consistency of the quality and the design of the product have allowed our company to thrive. Other companies in our industry seem to come and go, but we've had longevity, driven largely by a commitment to not disappoint the consumer.

We are in a few different businesses: the juvenile business, the gift business, and the business of celebrating occasions. Each one has a different profile and a different set of expectations. To ensure that the company generates revenue and profit, we try to stay abreast of consumer needs and attitudes, and general demographic and demand cycle information relative to these different businesses. We tend to be very sensitive to what the consumer-level attitudes are for those particular categories.

We also have exceptionally close relationships with the trade, and a great deal of respect for our customers' opinions of where the market is going and what the market requires. Being a good listener to your customers' read of the marketplace helps you to better gauge what the market demand is and partner with them in assessing and delivering content against it.

Overcoming Challenges

Sometimes challenges arise that are beyond our control, such as material costs. Much of what we create is in the area of cut-and-sewn products, and those are often made out of polyester materials that are ultimately an oil-based derivative. As a result of what's been going on in the oil industry lately, there have been some real pressures on our business to deliver the same level of quality at the same price when our raw material prices are rising substantially.

There are also expansion and growth pain challenges, primarily related to China, the country of origin on many of our products. With the rapid expansion and industrialization of China, it is a challenge to find the appropriate number of individuals to fill positions in many of the factories, and then there are pressures relative to energy supply to keep those factories operating on a forty- or fifty-hour-a-week basis. The expansion has been so fast and widespread that it has outstripped the development of infrastructure to support it.

Other challenges relate to the changing distribution patterns within the marketplace and the increased challenge to the independent retailer to compete with the larger mass merchandising organizations. The challenge for us is to develop a unique value proposition that works well for each channel so we have product in both channels.

Determining a Profitable Product Mix

We determine our product mix largely in conjunction with our retail partners. We work pretty closely with them, relative to the size and scope of certain brands; a lot of what we do is brand-driven. There needs to be a certain minimum level of coverage within a brand matrix, and very often we'll start with a matrix that covers various categories or subcategories within the brand at various price points. We tend to look at a matrix in the present, and ensure that we have the various price points and categories covered, which is often the major driving force in determining the depth of the line. Then we look at the lifecycles of the products within that matrix on an annualized basis, and we continually assess where a product is in its lifecycle, and when it's time to retire a product and replace it with something else.

In attempting to take away shelf space from a competing product, we have to understand the retailer's requirements. We then make a case to the retailer that a product we have can outperform a competitor's product already on the shelf. It boils down to understanding the retailer's expectations in terms of productivity per square or linear foot, and presenting a proposition that convinces them that our product can outperform whatever it is we are trying to replace.

The amount of profit we want to make varies with each product, depending upon what the market will bear. We have operating expenses to cover, and we like to see margins that bring us in at the 45 or 50 percent level on average, so we can cover our operating expenses and make a little bit of a profit for our shareholders.

We perpetually review profitable products and value engineer them, ensuring that they are contemporary with current market demands. It could be something as simple as changing the color, material, or another aesthetic aspect of a product to make it more updated. Some products don't require any changes; they are just perennial staples that stand the test of time. We insist that our brand managers constantly assess the validity of a product within the marketplace, regardless of how long it's been around. It's important to always look at the competition and the market demand, and adapt accordingly.

A financially successful product is one that delivers to both the retailer and to us a level of profit that supports the initial investment. A successful product has a reasonable lifecycle so that once the cost of the product's market entry is covered, higher margins are earned in subsequent years. If a product appears to be an excellent value to the consumer, then it's successful. Achieving this has much to do with the longevity of a company or a brand.

Keeping the Edge with Customers

To keep an edge with customers, I get into the stores and talk to my customers. We do formal consumer testing such as focus groups, or sometimes we'll actually put small quantities of products into market testing at retail locations. In addition, we do a lot of kitchen marketing. Ultimately, all of us have a lot of associates, friends, and family, and we tend to query them as to what their sentiments are regarding things we are doing, things our competition is doing, and what's working and not working in the marketplace.

Attaining and Measuring Success

To ensure that our company executes, we hold employees accountable. Each level of management within the business has specific objectives, and we hold people accountable to those objectives in terms of their performance reviews, their compensation, and everything else that goes along with it.

Success in any business ultimately comes in the form of what value you add to your business. The true test of a business is when you roll up from an item to a brand to a portfolio of brands to an umbrella brand, to the point where from year to year, the perceived value increases, and it's reflected in the amount of content you move into the market. You hope it shows a growth pattern in the amount of profit you make as a company and in the value of your shares. We're a publicly traded company, so in our case the ultimate objective is to make sure our shareholders receive the appropriate level of return on their investment in our business.

Industry Change

In the last five to ten years, the changes in our industry have been driven by consumer purchasing patterns. Today, people look for respectable value, and they want a seamless shopping experience. They don't have a lot of time to shop, so it's very important that your product's message is very, very clear at the point of sale and through your advertising.

Distribution has also changed. Since people don't have a lot of time to shop anymore, they tend to shop at places where they can get a lot accomplished in a relatively small period of time. As a result, you have to make sure your products are represented in those kinds of venues as well as traditional ones. Examples are specialty stores (card and gift, high-end drug, department stores) versus mass channels (national discount chains, drug chains, grocery stores). It's important to be sensitive to what the consumer is saying to marketers: Give me something where I get the joke in a hurry, and where you make it as simple as possible for me to understand, find, and buy the product.

Andrew R. Gatto was appointed president and chief executive officer of Russ Berrie and Company Inc. in June of 2004. Mr. Gatto has more than thirty years of experience in the toy industry, most recently as senior vice president of product development, imports, and strategic sourcing for Toys "R" Us in Wayne, New Jersey. He began his career at Toys "R" Us in 1998. There, Mr. Gatto created two of the company's most successful brands, Animal Alley Plush and Home Depot Tools, and established a global private brands division.

Prior to joining Toys "R" Us, Mr. Gatto served as president and chief executive officer of V-Tech Industries' Play-Tech division and Matchbox Toys North America. He has also held senior management positions with Toy Biz, LJN Toys, Durham Industries, and Fisher Price Toys. During his tenure at Toy Biz, Mr. Gatto grew the business from $65 million to more than $300 million; the company was cited by Fortune *magazine as one of America's 200 best run public companies.*

At LJN Toys in New York, Mr. Gatto grew the business from $55 million to $280 million, primarily through entertainment-based licenses (Worldwide Wrestling Federation and Disney) and through acquisitions of niche companies such as Entertech Toys and THQ Electronics.

Mr. Gatto and his wife, Susan, reside in Saddle River and have three children.

Dedication: *To the late Russ Berrie and his uncompromising commitment to create quality products that make people smile.*

Paradigm Shift: Marketing Socially Responsible Products

John Bellamy

Chairman and Chief Executive Officer

The Knockout Group Inc.

A Vision for the Consumer Products Industry

The Knockout Group is a strategically integrated global marketing company committed to the development of celebrity-branded products that are safe for human use and environmentally friendly.

Our company's mission statement, as stated above, is the foundation for the philosophy and core values that drive the way we do business, treat our associates, and approach the marketplace. Our vision for the consumer products industry is that consumer product companies will listen to consumers and bring products to the marketplace in an efficient and responsible manner. The key word here is responsible: too many companies are creating and marketing products that are not safe or environmentally friendly. In spite of a world threatened by global warming, massive weather changes, and diminishing resources, they have simply not entered into the daily consciousness of most consumer product companies. The ultimate goal of these companies should be to provide efficacy and convenience without harm.

What Consumer Products Companies Need to Succeed

Because of the nature of the world today, technology is often the driver in creating or improving products. Thus, technology and the ability to adapt to it are clearly components that belong at the top of the list for any company that wants to be successful. Whether it is a matter of the ingredients, the formulation, or the delivery mechanism, technology is the penultimate tool. However, human desire is the prime force that must be reckoned with in bringing a product to market. No matter how technologically advanced it is, a product will not succeed if there is no demand for its intrinsic benefits.

Finally, true success comes from keeping your ear to the ground and never failing to listen to the consumer. One mistake that even the most successful of companies can make is to rest on its laurels. Companies often feel that because they have established a historic position in the marketplace, they are inviolate to consumer whim. These companies have made incredibly costly mistakes that prove this is not so. A corporation must remain vigilant and dynamic in order to succeed.

Industry Challenges

One of the greatest challenges in this industry, as well as for any business that is consumer-focused, is finding the proper balance among what people want, what they need, how they want it delivered, and how much they are willing to pay for it.

In our particular segment—delivering consumer products to the general consumer market—we must remind ourselves everyday that our products often do not represent basic needs. People *need* food; they simply have to have it or they will die. People also need cleaning products, but such products are expendable when there is no money in the wallet to pay for them. To me, that makes for an even greater challenge.

Because we have an evolutionary product that requires some amount of education in order to gain consumer appreciation and acceptance, we have to pursue our marketing challenge in creative ways. The short form commercial does not work for us and, even if we were extraordinarily cash rich, we would not want to position ourselves via the typical mass media channels. Thirty seconds during the commercial break on "Desperate Housewives" is not what will sell Knockout products. We need a vehicle that enables us to provide information that will encourage an informed consumer. This is the trigger we believe will change generational preferences and help us ascend to a leadership position in the marketplace.

Another challenge is the issue of consumer complacency. Our research has shown that consumers often follow buying patterns that are based upon what is already familiar to them. These are often inherited preferences based on the choices their parents made and taught to them from childhood. Very often, their choices have nothing to do with what is best for them as individuals. These emotional purchases can continue for generation after generation until something happens that triggers a change.

Our approach is to empower consumers, not only with knowledge of our products and their attributes, but via an appeal to quality of life interests. Our greatest aspiration, therefore, is bringing about a change in consumer behavior that may be deeply entrenched from years of habit.

The single biggest challenge we face, in a word, is pull-through. We are like one little David competing in a marketplace crowded with Goliaths. Our competitors spend huge sums, often up to $80 million, for each and every product they launch. They are rewarded with immediate product recognition and concomitant sales. We do not have the budgets to compete at that level, so we are constantly challenged to find innovative ways to gain trial. We believe that once consumers try our products, they will quickly become loyal to our brand because of its benefits and differentiation.

Deciding on the Right Product Mix

Largely, the right product mix depends on consumer demand. Our fundamental position is that consumers are not only ready but asking for products that are healthy and environmentally friendly—but not at a sacrificial price.

An example of a new product offering would be our response to the huge success of the George Foreman Grill, a product marketed by Salton Products. Other than the fact of George Foreman's involvement, Salton is unrelated to Knockout in any way. However, their huge success with marketing the George Foreman Grill, which has sold more than 70 million units, led us to create a George Foreman Knockout Grill Cleaner. Our goal was to capitalize on what should be obvious consumer interest.

Among the many benefits of the Knockout Grill Cleaner is that it is non-toxic, safe around children and pets, and free of chemical residue. In addition to all these great benefits, it still delivers cleaning efficiency.

For us, the right product mix is one that relies on line extensions in categories that are either not oversaturated or where there is an obvious unmet need. We are not a mature enough company to have a position on when to lose products. Our optimism about what we do, which is supported by solid research, tells us that our products will have a very long life indeed. In comparison to competing brands, we are confident that many generations of customer satisfaction lie ahead. Taking items off the roster is not something worth consideration at this point.

Product Expenses

It is ironic that the least expensive elements in our production equation are the ingredients that go into making our products. All of the ingredients are natural materials that are found generously in nature. An example would be the thyme (the same herb used in cooking) that is used to formulate our Knockout Disinfectant. It has been registered with the Environmental Protection Agency, kills 99.99 percent of bacteria, is safe for use on food contact surfaces and children's toys, and unlike competitive disinfectants, requires no cautions or warnings on the product labels.

It is important to note that we contract our manufacturing; therefore, the category in which we spend the most money is marketing. Even though the marketing is the most expensive part, we try to do it smartly and efficiently so that it does not have a deleterious impact on pricing.

The Importance of Quality Customer Service

Our primary customers are the retailers that deliver our products to the end user: the consumer. Not only must we deliver a supply of products, we have to drive demand so consumers will come looking for us on the shelves of the retailers. It is only when our shipments sell out time and time again that we have done our job effectively and made our customers happy enough for both us and the retailers to make money. That means we have to provide an exceptional level of customer service.

A good deal of our customer service is based on face-to-face contact. Our sales team will sell products and then roam the aisles to talk to consumers, get competitive intelligence, and mine for promotional ideas.

Because we see our commerce as a partnership, we are always listening and trying to find ways for everyone to participate as an active player in the marketing program. A good example would be the largest retailer in the world, a company that has single-handedly redefined the entire retail industry. They are very specific about what they want and how they want it delivered. They are also very savvy about how to sell the product on an internal level so their employees are excited about it and will help move it off the shelves. We are learning their system from bottom to top, and we try to anticipate what they might ask of us so we can give it to them before the request comes in. With a client like this, their wish is our command.

Listening to Your Audience: How to Incorporate Market and Customer Feedback

We are very aggressive in our efforts to understand our markets. The data we collect from focus groups, research, and customers is reflected in our branding, customer relations management, and product development.

When we recently conducted focus groups, some of the results were surprising. Naturally, we entered the process with certain preconceived notions about a product and what it means to the consumer. With this in mind, we witnessed several startling revelations that added even more depth to our marketing strategy. One of the biggest findings was that consumers were not consciously aware that it was possible to have a product that both cleaned well and was safe for the family, pets, and the environment—and, on top of that, even smelled good.

We proceeded to integrate those learning's into our marketing strategy and eventually decided to change our product labels and re-launch our cleaning systems. The information we learned from the consumers took a primary position in our marketing message.

Keeping the Edge with Respect to Your Customer Base

Because our primary customer is the retailer, we stay abreast of what is happening in that industry. In America, retail is an industry that used to be pretty stable; however, with the emergence of discounters and a demonstrated preference, even by the wealthy, for value shopping, the industry is irrevocably changing. These changes will have great impact on consumer product companies.

Our biggest source of information is the customers themselves. They are quick to point out what we need to do to help propel their and our business, because to do so creates a win-win situation. We also do a lot of reading. Publications from Aspatore Books are extremely helpful in this regard, as are industry reports and analyses from McKinsey and other heavyweight consulting firms.

We also attend trade shows and participate in conferences that directly relate to any and all aspects of our business.

Following Through: Making Sure the Company Executes

At Knockout, we have an extremely capable management team that has never yet disappointed us. The members of this team are drawn from a variety of disciplines and industries, and have found the synergy to be able to work effectively as a group. If someone is not pulling their weight, I have no doubt that it would be instantly obvious to all involved; as the chairman, I am neither the only nor the most important observer of performance. Further, as a publicly held company, our board of directors is intimately involved in all aspects of the business and continually provides us with the benefit of their experience and oversight.

Measuring Success: Benchmarks

Our company will be successful as long as we maintain an environment that is conducive to success. We are only slightly over two years old and, already, we have distribution in 80 percent of American markets. We succeeded in going public and capitalizing our venture to an astonishing degree in a record amount of time, which says we must be doing something right.

The tangible gauge of success is our profitability and the return on investment we bring to our stakeholders. To achieve that, we believe we have to make sound decisions and work smartly to achieve our goals. It is not the amount of money we spend on marketing that engenders success, but how intelligently we plan market entry and management. We consider our products to be successful if they deliver the benefits we promise to the consumer.

Industry Changes Over the Past Years

Over the past decade, branded products have weathered many storms. In a mature market like America, where everyone has equal access to education and advertising, it is very hard to distinguish oneself on a crowded shelf. Add to that the incredible growth of discounters, who are able to offer even premium brands at lower than competitive prices, and you have a very daunting market indeed.

Almost universally, major consumer products companies survived the last decade by concentrating on core brands, eliminating waste, and improving productivity. As a result, according to *The McKinsey Quarterly*, "Anyone who invested every year since 1993 in the top fifty consumer goods companies (minus the tobacco companies, whose shares were affected by liability lawsuits) received a 12 percent annual return over ten years—results that outperformed those of most industry sectors. Eight of the top ten companies of 1993 (ranked by sales) were still in the list of leaders in 2003, and roughly in the same order."

Private labels and discount retailing continue to be threatening, but intelligent marketers are responding with a shift of paradigm. On the private label issue, alliances between discount retailers and manufacturers has created new niches so that both private label and premium brands occupy the same shelf, both racking up impressive results at the cash register without cannibalizing one another.

At Knockout, we see a path forward in delivering added value to cost-conscious consumers who are growing concerned about personal health and environmental issues. Our business model relies on outsourcing our production so we do not have to invest heavily in capital equipment or warehouse space. Our main expertise is marketing and building relationships that propel sales, both with consumers and the retailers who put our products into their hands. We believe that maintaining our focus, being in tune with consumer preferences, and being able to turn on a dime will be what help us negotiate the rocky waters that lie ahead.

Changes Over the Next Five to Ten Years

Over the next decade, the changing demographics of American society, in addition to the continued emergence of new markets in the global universe and an increasingly pressurized competition on the price/value continuum, will continue to impact business worldwide. These impacts will be felt inordinately in the consumer products category.

At Knockout, we believe these dynamics are positive. We are preparing ourselves to respond to changing demographics by creating products with universal appeal and marketing them with careful attention to the cultural nuances of all of our market segments. We are also positioning ourselves to expand globally, choosing our markets with great care based on an intention to enter at the "magic moment" when the market is mature enough to appreciate the tangible personal benefits of products such as ours. By being smart managers and marketers, we feel we will be well positioned to serve the price/value mandate. In fact, we see ourselves bridging the gap between product efficacy and environmental sensitivity in a way that will help propel masses of people to invest in the earth's future by purchasing products that are efficacious in their homes.

Industry Advice

I think the most important thing for everyone involved with our company to remember is that *we* are the consumer. Before we are marketers, we are normal human beings with families and home lives. The basic intelligence we garner in our everyday private lives can have substantial application in what we do professionally. A recent example of this is that during a management meeting concerning the development cycle for a recent product, we realized that all of our family members always wear gloves when cleaning with chemical products. We explored further and found that the reason for the gloves was related to the harshness of the products. The profound simplicity of this seemingly universal act quickly became crystal clear and provided our marketing team with an insight that could be integrated into the planning of our marketing message. Knockout offers products that not only deliver on the cleaning promise, but are so safe that no gloves are required.

In turn, the best advice I have ever received is to know your industry, stay true to your mission statement, and market your products responsibly.

Golden Rules for Success

There are four golden rules upon which Knockout is relying for success:

- Superior product and packaging,
- Innovation through technology and partnership,
- Outstanding customer relationship management, and
- Creative marketing expertise and realization.

We believe following these tenets will empower us to meet the needs and desires of consumers, ultimately proving beneficial for all involved.

John Bellamy is founder, chairman, and chief executive officer of the Knockout Group Inc., exclusive licensee to manufacture and distribute a line of environmentally friendly automotive and household cleaning products globally branded by George Foreman. Mr. Bellamy is a visionary entrepreneur with more than twenty-five years experience in various facets of business with an emphasis on consumer products, particularly from brand development through media production and placement. Fortune 500 relationships and experiences include McDonald's, NBC, FOX, Kraft, Wal-Mart and General Electric. He is a highly motivated executive, adept problem solver, and perceptive in a variety of marketing and production areas.

Previously Mr. Bellamy was executive vice president of Dick Gregory Health Enterprises Inc. a weight control and health maintenance organization. He acted as Dick Gregory's business manager and chief officer of the corporation. He successfully negotiated a $100 million contract with a multinational corporation to market a line of nutritional products. Mr. Bellamy organized, designed, and implemented a mail order operation and established independent distributors across the United States to market the product line, including books and video cassettes.

Mr. Bellamy was named outstanding trainee in the United States Army and is a Vietnam War veteran, serving from 1967 to 1969, who received the Purple Heart. He has received the Governor's Award for the Arts, has been listed in Who's Who in Finance and Industry and Who's Who in America, and has received the Inspiration to Youth Community Achievement Award.

Dedication: *To Katie Bellamy, my dedicated and supportive partner. Angela, LaTasha, Sheena, Ymani, and Caleb, the bright lights of my life. My dad, Bishop John Bellamy, who encouraged me to never give up. My mom, for her tireless nurturing, spiritual counseling, and love. Sharon Morgan, E.dali Pollard, and Abiiba Howell for assistance in making this a reality.*

Creating Value through Innovation in Consumer Products

Jeff M. Fettig
Chairman of the Board, President, and Chief Executive Officer
Whirlpool Corporation

A Vision for the Consumer Products Industry

The Pathway to Success

The key to success in the consumer products industry is inherent in the vision of our company: a fundamental belief that we can build customer loyalty for our brands by providing unique consumer solutions to meet consumer needs. Our view is that you cannot provide unique solutions unless you truly have an innovative company. Innovation has played an essential role in our strategy over the last several years.

Our company's vision is "Every Home...Everywhere." It is based on the fact that we have been globalizing our company for a number of years. We are in the consumer space, primarily in home appliances. Fundamentally, we believe we can effectively meet consumers' needs around the world in 170 different markets. Twenty years ago, we were primarily a United States-based company. Today, our marketplace is any space within the home, and we define it as global. We created a specific vision, which defines our business as consumer spaces in the home.

Whirlpool Versus Other Companies

Historically, the appliance business has been viewed as a product and manufacturing business. It has a longer purchase cycle than what people traditionally think of as typical for consumer products. This is not fast-moving consumer goods; it is a purchasing process for a given product, which can be eight to ten years. We have a very different opinion; we believe it is a consumer business, not a product manufacturing business.

Our brand value creation strategy is unique in comparison with the strategies of other companies in our industry. In our strategy, there are three fundamental elements with which we must do extraordinarily well worldwide in order for us to succeed and create value. The first element is having the best cost and quality position (global operating platform). We have cost-competitive products and strong productivity capabilities throughout our company. Quality is the heritage we originally built our company on, and it is still an essential attribute. Many companies run their business solely on this axis.

The second important factor for success is trade position and trade management (trade partner platform). We sell more than 44 million appliances each year. Virtually 100 percent of these appliances are sold through trade partners, whether they are retailers, builders, trade distributors, or other trade partners. Consequently, it is very important that we do a great job of aligning our strategy with the strategies of our trade partners, ensuring that we build strong partnerships. We must have a very solid business-to-business capability so we can serve our partners efficiently and address their needs. Again, other companies can replicate this trade position, but this factor alone is not sufficient for success.

The third factor, our best consumer position, truly differentiates us as a company (customer loyalty platform). We are focused on building customer loyalty for our brands. Our orientation to the business is to see through the eyes of the customer, understand their needs and wants, discover what is working and not working, and develop true insights. That insight, which we focus through a brand lens, is targeted at distinct consumer segments. Then we are able to apply our innovation skills to develop unique solutions, whether it is a product solution or service solution. This has been our formula for growth.

Although there are other companies in this industry that have succeeded at some elements of our success formula, our integrated approach of understanding the dynamics of the global business and driving it through the consumer's eyes sets us apart from other companies.

The consumer aspect is the hardest piece, but it has the biggest payoff. Building company capabilities has been our focus for a long time. We have a very specific approach to developing customer loyalty with our customers. Customer loyalty is measured by three predominate customer behaviors: 1) repurchasing the brand when it is time to replace, 2) creating an emotional link that leads to cross-purchases of other products (for example, from a washer to a dishwasher), and 3) ultimately creating passionate brand ambassadors who recommend the brand to others who cross-purchase.

This definition of customer loyalty sets the bar very high. Given this strict definition, our goal is to double customer loyalty in ten years.

Brand Customer Loyalty is a Behavior

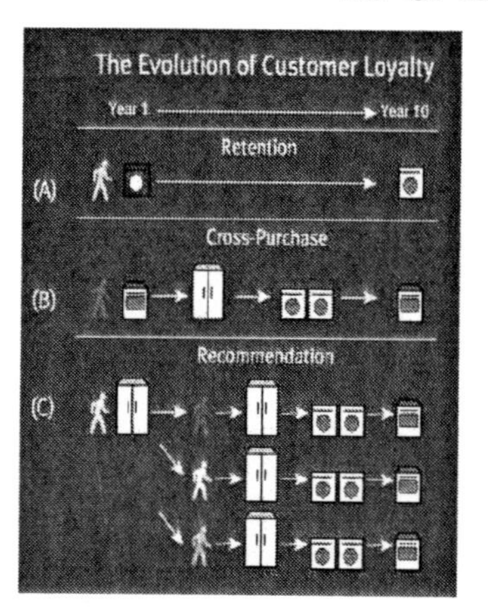

A) Loyalty is more than repurchasing the same brand when it is time to replace.
B) Loyalty creates an emotional link that leads to cross-purchases of other products.
C) Loyalty ultimately creates passionate brand ambassadors that recommend the brand to others who cross-buy.

We measure Loyalty in every key market in the world.

Generating Revenue and Profits

Fundamentally, the key to generating revenue and profits rests in having an intense understanding of customer needs and opportunities. Clearly, our products have to be competitive. There is a natural growth in the business globally of about 3 percent from a unit standpoint. From a revenue standpoint, we have seen a long period of price deflation. However, we have a strategy of not competing on price; our value proposition is based on innovation.

We use innovation to drive revenue growth, to change historical dynamics, and to create new spaces in the marketplace. If you look at our core products, you will see that we have been able to build new revenue pools and bases around them by understanding customer needs and wants, and we have extended our business from our traditional core appliance business into other avenues.

Products

Our focus on the consumer determines the makeup of our product lines. The consumer tells us what to do, and the mix of our business reflects the needs and wants of the different segments of the market. We continue to connect with consumers by producing brands that focus on distinct customer segments. For example, in our North American business, our key brands are:

Brand	**Segment**	**Brand Promise**
KitchenAid	Home Enthusiast	Bringing legendary performance to help her achieve home and culinary dreams
Whirlpool	Active Balancer	Imaginative solutions that help her be incredibly productive
Kenmore* *Sears-Owned	All American Mom	Peace of mind for her family

We have a range of returns on different products. With the capital nature of our business, typically you need to target an 8 to 10 percent operating profit in order to return the cost of capital. The most expensive part of the process is material and components, which are approximately 70 percent of our cost basis. Given this, how we design, produce, and market products and services are based on customer needs, not just cost.

Market Share

When consumers purchase, they decide what represents the highest value to them. What determines value is a ratio of the benefits that a product or service provides versus cost. There are two ways to achieve a higher ratio: one is cost-based, and the other is a higher perceived benefit through innovation. Our view from a cost price standpoint is that we have to be competitive; it is the ante to play in the game. The point that differentiates us from our competitors is that we typically grow our business and market share based on offering unique solutions from a brand innovation perspective.

Innovation

Before five years ago, one could argue that there hadn't really been a new innovation in our industry for the last fifteen to twenty years. Innovation has to meet three different sets of criteria at Whirlpool. The first is that it has to be a unique solution currently not available to a consumer. The second criterion is that the innovation cannot be easily duplicated by competitors. Lastly, the innovation has to have an above-average return on investment. This strict criterion drives true innovation. If we change a handle on a door, it is not going to be called innovation because it does not meet all three of the criteria. But when we introduce a sink that is also a dishwasher, as we did with the KitchenAid Briva, we have met all three of the innovation criteria. Again, we are setting our bar very high and defining innovation from the consumer's standpoint.

We introduced an average of eight new products or services per year between 2001 and 2003 that fit our strict criteria. This year, we are introducing fourteen. Next year, we will introduce nineteen projects. We continue to accelerate the pace of innovation into the marketplace. We have over 500 project innovations in our pipeline that will ultimately have to meet our criteria; or else they won't make it through our pipeline.

Herb,

I thought you would enjoy the "wonder" in this book. Arthur and his wife, Pamela, live next door,

All best

Carol Hoffman

David Henderson

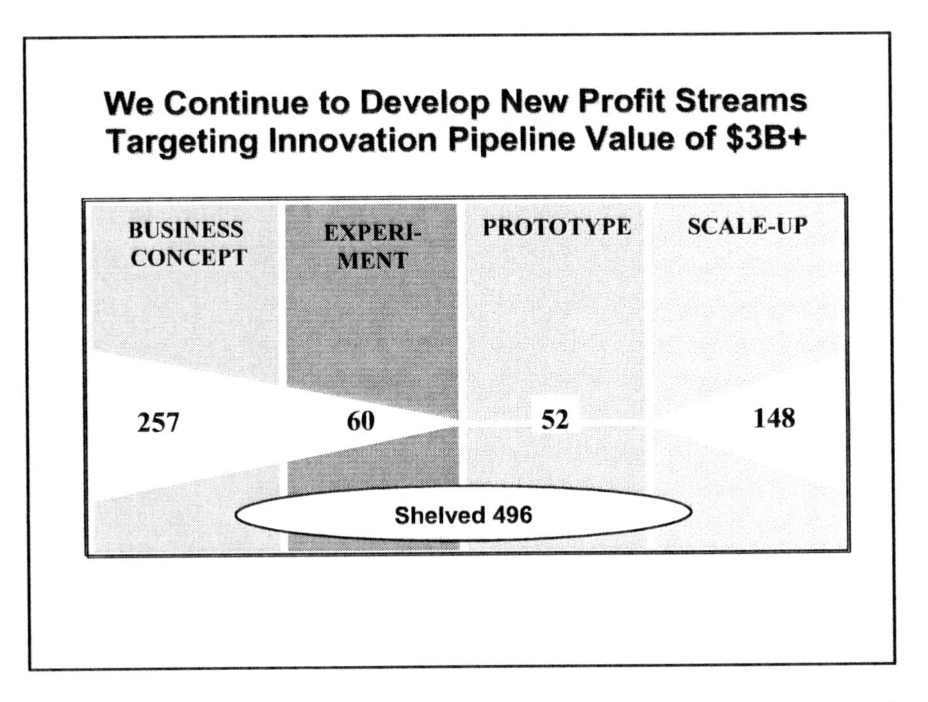

The starting point is to understand what you have and that there is a need to refresh that product, and then you must use a number of tools to build customer loyalty. Advertising and point of sale with our trade partners are two such tools. We increasingly advertise on the trade partners' floor. We have also increased our direct contact with consumers through the Internet. More and more people are using these tools to see what is available when they are in the market.

Execution

Execution depends on a number of different facets. Our management process starts with goal development across the company. Creating consistent alignment across and up and down the company is essential. We reinforce it with a performance management process, which is the way we set goals and measure people's performance. We have daily, weekly, monthly, quarterly, and annual management processes during which we review performance metrics very closely with all of the operating units around the world. We compare these actual metrics to the plan. Based on this information, we make adjustments in our execution. Another important area is training and development. You execute better if you have great people with the right capabilities that enable them to execute. Lastly, we have an ongoing process of benchmarking competitors and other industries to understand their level of execution. As we gather this information, we bring that knowledge back into our management processes and capability building.

Setting Goals

Setting goals starts with creating value. We are a publicly traded, share-held company, and we believe our first obligation is to create value for shareholders, customers, and employees. Fundamentally, our goals are built upon the returns we believe we should get based on our capabilities and the resources invested in the business. We sort through various ideas and figure out how to make them viable propositions for our customers. From there, we formulate long-term, medium-term, and short-term goals. This ongoing process never ends; it is always updated, revisited, and changed if things in the environment change. Setting goals is a management process we have incorporated into our quarterly, annual, and strategic planning. Our growth rates and our ability to generate returns are demonstrating that this industry is an exciting space and a good investment category.

Thought Leadership

Whirlpool Strategies

Our company has been a leader in globalization since the late 1980s. We identified the elements of our industry as being global, and we were on the leading edge of executing that strategy. We had a presence in the critical markets around the world, and we were able to transform into a globally integrated company. It is clear that we led the process of globalization in our industry. One of our other strategies has been to make a big shift from a product manufacturing orientation to a brand-consumer orientation, which has led to our brand-customer loyalty strategy. We have focused upon seeing through the eyes of the customer as opposed to the eyes of the manufacturer. Over the last four to five years, we have shifted toward building innovation as a fundamental capability of the business. All three of these strategies have differentiated our company from others in the industry.

Generating New Ideas

As we embarked upon a true consumer strategy a number of years ago, we felt that innovation had to become a core competency in our company. This wouldn't be accomplished with just a few engineers or a few smart people to think up new ideas. Instead, we needed innovation from "Everyone and Everywhere." We have approached this as building a fundamental capability within our company. We have trained thousands of people, and we have certification processes for people who have been trained in innovation tools. We have realigned our systems and processes to support innovation. A big part of our compensation is built around delivering innovation to the marketplace, so we have incorporated innovation into our business processes so that our ideas are really coming from hundreds if not thousands of people across the company. Both formal and informal teams are motivated and rewarded to work on innovation.

Major Changes

Globalization and the speed of change have increased significantly in the consumer products industry in recent years. The rate of change is growing at a faster rate all the time. This was not an innovative industry five to ten years ago, but we are driving it to become one. In the future, the speed of change will continue to accelerate. Additionally, there will be continued global consolidation of companies within our industry. There will be some big winners, and many companies will not succeed.

Golden Rules

The consumer products industry is an exciting growth industry with a wide open space for innovation. We are starting to see the positive impacts of innovation across our marketplace worldwide. One example of this is our successful Duet washer and dryer. In a market where five years ago a washer's average price was $399, we introduced a $1,200 washer with higher performance and innovative styling. The consumer reaction to the Duet has been extraordinary, and it is now the number-one selling product at a price that is three times the average. If you execute well, stay innovative, and completely understand customer needs, you can grow and earn high returns.

Industry Advice

There is a common perception that the consumer products industry is a slow growth industry. However, we believe there are ample opportunities for significant growth. It is only a slow growth industry if you let yourself think it is. Another important thing to remember is the importance of creating value in the eyes of the consumer. I was told early on in my career about the significance of the value of our products. If we don't believe there is value in our products, why should anyone else? The following caution rings true in the consumer products industry: "It takes two seconds to reduce your price and two years to get it back." No competitor has a sustainable advantage in a price-driven approach. The best way to succeed is to develop great brands and innovative products and services for which consumers will pay a fair price and, in turn, enables you to create value.

Jeff M. Fettig was named Whirlpool Corporation's chairman, president, and chief executive officer in July of 2004. He served as president and chief operating officer, as well as on Whirlpool's board of directors, from June of 1999.

Mr. Fettig joined Whirlpool in 1981 as an operations associate. He held a number of managerial positions in operations, sales, planning, and product development before being promoted to vice president of marketing for the KitchenAid Appliance Group in July of 1989. In October of 1990, he was named vice president of marketing for the Philips Whirlpool Appliance Group of Whirlpool Europe B.V., the company's European subsidiary, and was named vice president of group marketing and sales for North American Appliance Group in October of 1992. In 1994, he was named an executive vice president of Whirlpool, and president of Whirlpool Europe and Asia.

A native of Tipton, Indiana, Mr. Fettig holds a bachelor's degree in finance and a master of business administration degree from Indiana University.
Mr. Fettig is a member of the board of directors of the Dow Chemical Company. He also serves as a national trustee of Boys & Girls Clubs of America–Midwest Region, and serves on the dean's advisory council of Indiana University.

Whirlpool Corporation is the world's leading manufacturer and marketer of major home appliances, with annual sales of more than $13 billion, 68,000 employees, and nearly fifty manufacturing and technology research centers around the globe. The company markets Whirlpool, KitchenAid, Brastemp, Bauknecht, Consul, and other major brand names to consumers in more than 170 countries.

The Formula for Success in the Lodging Industry

Stephen H. Marcus
Chairman and Chief Executive Officer
The Marcus Corporation

The Basics of the Lodging Industry

The lodging industry got its start with people opening up their homes for weary travelers. That basic concept is the same today, with accommodations ranging from a simple room (the economy segment) to exceptional properties in the full-service hotels and resorts segment, offering exquisitely decorated rooms, fabulous restaurants, luxurious spas, golf courses, fitness centers, and many other amenities.

But regardless of the property type, the formula for success revolves around average daily occupancy and average daily room rate. The goal is to rent the room and provide the amenities at a cost that pays the expenses and provides a fair return on investment. Within that framework, we like to provide the little extras that make people feel they got more than their money's worth.

There are three primary types of operators in the industry:

- Companies that own and operate their own branded properties
- Companies that franchise their brand to others
- Franchisees who own and operate a property under another company's "flag"

There are companies that are a combination. For example, some companies own and operate some properties and also franchise their brand to others. In some cases, our company will partner with others in providing the equity while we assume the responsibility for managing a property. And some franchisees own and operate properties for a variety of franchisors.

The Marcus Corporation Vision

Our company's vision is based on the philosophies of my father, who founded the Marcus Corporation back in 1935. He believed in providing quality, service, and value. He believed that our associates are our greatest asset because, as he said, "You can have all the managers you want, but the day the maintenance person doesn't show up to sweep the floors, you know how important every associate is to the company." He also believed in owning the company's real estate rather than leasing. Owning the vast majority of our assets adds stability to our operations and provides opportunities to maximize shareholder value over the long term. Finally, he believed that every business must provide a reasonable return on investment for the company's shareholders.

We're a smaller player in lodging and compete every day against giants such as Marriott, Hilton, and others. We've carved out a niche by building a diverse and distinctive portfolio of properties.

Because of our size, we have the ability to pay attention to details and develop the unique attributes of each property. For example, we are experts at renovating and operating historic hotels. The Pfister Hotel in Milwaukee, the Hilton Milwaukee City Center, and the Hotel Phillips in Kansas City, are all unique and distinctive properties that are the leading historic hotels in their markets.

Overall, I believe our focus on managing for the long term is a major distinguishing factor for the Marcus Corporation. We invest in our properties and maintain them, in both good times and bad. After September 11, many lodging companies pulled back and cut maintenance and capital expenditures. We didn't, because we believe that if just one guest notices a frayed carpet or a faded bedspread, we've waited too long to replace it. So we continually reinvest in our properties to keep them fresh and new, and to keep our guests coming back again and again.

Creating a Unique Experience

In the lodging business, the guest experience is everything. We don't have a tangible product. Our guests don't leave with a pair of shoes or a new coat; they leave with memories of their stay. We want their stay to be everything they expected it to be—and more. That's where our associates come in. They are the ones who make our guests' experience the best it can be.

Creating a unique experience comes down to knowing your customers and knowing your market. We are constantly monitoring trends in customer preferences. We also look at the competition and think of how we can be unique and on the leading edge of new trends.

For example, we saw the growing interest among families in water parks and built an indoor water park at our historic Hilton Milwaukee City Center. This is the only indoor water park in downtown Milwaukee, and as a result the hotel, which is primarily a convention center hotel, has increased its weekend business.

Our guests' experience stands out because of the unique properties we have. We're not starting from a cookie-cutter room but from a distinctive property with unique attributes. Around that, we build the amenities and services that fit the location and the customer base. And, of course, public relations and marketing are how we inform people of what we have to offer. Our challenge in marketing is that we don't have the economies of scale of the large chains—yet we still need to be visible and attract new guests. We have increased our visibility by participating on Web sites such as Hotels.com and Expedia. We also do a lot of public relations focusing on the properties and our amenities. We consider public relations and advertising to be investments in building and maintaining our market share, and encouraging new guests to try our properties.

From our point of view, the ideal guest experience would be one in which the guest is greeted warmly upon entering the property. He or she would receive a warm welcome at the registration desk. The room would be ready, spotlessly cleaned, with everything in place. Our staff would assist the guest with sightseeing and other activities, and the individual's experience in our restaurants and service areas would be equally flawless. Or, if there were a problem, it would be handled quickly and to the guest's satisfaction.

Greatest Challenges

The greatest challenges to the lodging business are the things you can't control that affect occupancy. Weather, the economy, and gasoline prices are typical factors. But in today's world, the biggest threat is terrorism. I've been in this business for forty years, and I had never seen an event with the impact of September 11th. Travel simply shut down; in the nearly three years since then, it has come back, but the industry still hasn't fully returned to where it was. Terrorism is a cloud hanging over the industry, because we know what impact another occurrence could have, and we're powerless to prevent it.

There are other challenges as well.

One aspect of our business that's different than others, such as retail, is that if a room isn't sold on a particular day, it's gone forever. We can't go back and sell it the next day. So we need to fill each room each and every day.

The Internet, as wonderful as it is for presenting our properties to prospective guests, also presents a challenge in terms of online booking at deep discounts. Some companies are willing to sell their rooms over the Internet at a substantially reduced rate just to get the occupancy. This puts pressure on everyone. And while it might build occupancy over the short term, over the long term it's a dangerous path to take. It's dangerous because once guests get accustomed to a lower rate it's hard to bump them back up to a higher one. Steeply discounted rates also don't provide for the ongoing maintenance that's needed to keep properties at their peak. So unless it's used very wisely, Internet booking at discounted rates can become a short-term solution that results in long-term problems.

Overbuilding is another challenge that periodically affects the industry. The story of the lodging industry is one of up and down cycles. Travel increases and there's a scarcity of rooms. So the hotel companies build more rooms to meet the demand. But everyone wants to jump on the bandwagon, so a lot of companies build a lot more rooms and in the end the supply exceeds the demand; until travel picks up again. And on and on it goes.

Low supply growth is great for owners of existing hotels like us who continually maintain and enhance their properties. Our goal is to be well positioned and ready to absorb increases in travel as they occur. And when there's an abundance of supply, our unique properties and outstanding amenities help to make our properties the first choice for our guests.

One challenge the lodging business shares with many others is the need to find enough skilled associates to operate and grow our business. Good, experienced people who have a positive attitude and want to grow with our company are always in demand. While technology is an effective tool, we're still in a people business, and to succeed we need talented associates who will take good care of our guests.

Achieving Financial Success

To be financially successful, of course, we need to bring in the revenues and we have to watch our expenses. This is a fine line, because regardless of the property, we have high standards for quality that we are committed to maintaining. Real estate is a key to success in this business. You have to have the right location to make a property work. We also need the discipline to maintain a strong balance sheet. We can't let debt get out of line. Our strong balance sheet gives us the ability to pursue opportunities that may come along and try new ideas and concepts to maintain our leading edge in our markets.

In this business, the rooms are the profit generator. The amenities, such as the food and beverage business, golf courses, spas, and other services, are the key to optimizing the guest rooms because they help differentiate the guest experience from the competition. In an urban setting, the only part of the hotel the local residents see is the lobby, the meeting rooms, and the restaurants and lounges. Local residents are a great referral source, so these amenities can leverage the guest rooms.

Our most profitable offerings are group events for which a group will not only book a block of rooms, but will also have banquet meals and activities such as golf tournaments and spa services.

Profitability differs by project. It's based on how much you have invested and the return you get on the investment. Revenue per available room (RevPAR) is the most important metric, but cost structure also enters into the equation. If you have a lower cost structure, you can still generate a good profit and a good return on investment.

Our biggest expense is personnel. Lodging is a labor-intensive business, from the front desk to room attendants to wait staff, and all of the other behind-the-scenes associates who make our guests' experience possible. In addition, utility costs have been increasing at a faster pace than in the past and, like everyone else, we are affected by rising health care costs.

The economy and time of year certainly affect revenues for our industry, as did September 11th, as mentioned above. We are also dependent upon events in each of the cities in which we operate. For example, the Harley-Davidson 100th anniversary celebration, which took place in Milwaukee in 2003, was great for our Milwaukee properties.

We are growing revenues by expanding our business. Our hotels and resorts division is focusing on adding management contracts that provide fee income without major capital investments. On the profitability side, we are using technology to our advantage to increase efficiency and reduce operating costs.

In terms of pricing, we use our technology to adjust the pricing to the demand. We maximize the rate potential when demand is high but then charge lower rates during slower periods. We also have loyal corporate customers whose rates we maintain as much as we can throughout the year. This is very common across the industry. Overall, however, we want to generate a fair return from each of our properties. After September 11th, many companies reduced their rates just to get people into their hotels to cover expenses. We wanted to maintain our rate integrity, because we were concerned that once we lowered the rates it would be difficult to get them back up again, and we might attract a customer base that would not move up to a higher price point at a later date. So we held fairly firm on rates and added value by creating packages that offered a free breakfast or other benefits that appealed to our guests but did not relate directly to the room rate.

The airlines were the first to create a pricing structure offering different prices during different seasons and different rates to different guests. It's the basic economic law of supply and demand. When there's a big convention in town and rooms are booked for a twenty-five-mile radius, of course you are going to charge a higher rate to balance January and February, which are very slow periods here in the Midwest.

As for the different rates for different guests, like any business we have some customers who do a higher volume of business with us than others. And like any business would, we give them a preferred rate, just as other types of businesses give volume discounts to their large customers. It also costs us less to service an account that is constantly giving us business than to set up a new account for each visit.

Company Culture

A wonderful aspect of the lodging business is the tradition it has of providing opportunities for people to build a career in the industry. Many young people work part-time at lodging businesses while they are in school. With the ongoing training many companies provide, they can advance within the company and grow into positions with increasing responsibility. There are also a number of colleges that offer degrees in hotel and restaurant management. Many of our managers have degrees from schools in the areas where we have operations. People know when a job is right for them, and in our industry it takes people who sincerely want to help others to enjoy a trip, a dinner, or a special event. My father said we are "people-pleasing people," and that statement is as true today as it was when he started the company nearly seventy years ago.

In adding new staff, we hire for attitude and train for everything else. For our managers, we also look for industry knowledge and experience, as well as honesty and integrity. We look for people who are a good fit for our culture and who share our philosophies. That said, we also look for people with an entrepreneurial spirit who aren't afraid to suggest new ideas and try new things to keep us on the leading edge.

Our culture is to give each division a great degree of autonomy. Of course, we review their strategic plans and budgets and approve their capital expenditures. We also have a return on investment that they are expected to generate. But within that framework, they have a fair amount of freedom to operate their business.

In 2003, we introduced a program called VMAX, which is an economic measurement tool that is the next step forward for us in tying management compensation to sustained improvement and profitability in each business. This makes our managers think like owners.

With everyone benefiting from the results of the division's operations, there is a great incentive to create an exceptional guest experience and keep guests returning again and again. All the associates know they have an important role in the guest experience, and that we are counting on them to do all they can to please our guests. We develop customer loyalty by being loyal to our associates. Taking good care of our associates translates into our associates taking good care of our guests.

There is no magic formula for excellent customer service. Customer service has many dimensions. We take frequent guest surveys and we read and respond to every letter we receive from a guest. We encourage our guests to tell us about their experience so we can continually work to make it better. I also keep the flow of information to my office as open as possible. If guests want to talk to me, they can. I'm a strong believer in accessibility.

We also watch the business. If you see a sudden drop that you can't account for, there's a good chance people aren't taking care of their customers. We also use the facilities ourselves, and we encourage our directors to use our facilities and file reports on their experience. I like to visit our properties and just walk around and talk to our associates. This gives me a chance to test associate attitudes and see our facilities in operation on a typical day.

There are many important behind-the-scenes tasks. Housekeeping, for example, is very important because cleanliness is the number-one criteria guests use in evaluating their stay. Reservations are also important, because a rude telephone receptionist could turn off a meeting planner organizing an event with $50,000 or $100,000 in revenues. While it may sound trite, the truth is that everyone is important to the success of our business.

Assessing Opportunities and Risks

In lodging, as in real estate, the key is location, location, location. But in addition to the location itself, we have to determine whether we can work the cost of the property and the improvements to develop a distinctive property that will also meet our objectives for return on investment. We look for locations with barriers to entry. They are more difficult to develop, but once they are built it is also more difficult for competitors to enter the market. We look at many opportunities, but we don't proceed unless they meet our criteria.

We also watch out for overbuilding, which happens in the lodging industry on a fairly regular cycle. Right now, the industry is overbuilt, but with the improvement in the economy and travel, room nights are catching up.

We put a great deal of effort into a potential opportunity up front to be certain that it will meet our expectations, and we take a conservative approach to developing our pro forma financials. We have sold a few properties that were financially marginal. If we're involved in a management contract that is not meeting our expectations, we do not renew it or we renegotiate with the owner.

In determining what risks are worth taking, we spend a lot of time on the groundwork. I like to walk the real estate and think about the property in terms of the project. We also sort out opportunities in terms of whether or not they meet our criteria. We want to maintain a strong balance sheet. Sometimes, we don't hit it exactly right, but we don't ever want to be in a position where one property can tip the balance sheet and put everything else at risk.

Changes and Trends in the Industry

The basic premise of the industry—providing lodging for business and leisure travelers—has not changed. What has changed is how you get those travelers into your properties. The Internet has had a major impact on this. The Web gives us a wonderful opportunity to showcase our properties and give our guests a feel for the property and its amenities. It also adds the convenience of online reservations for guests who prefer that method.

The Web also enables guests to compare properties and rates. The introduction of Web sites such as Hotels.com and Expedia provides another avenue for marketing to potential guests and obtaining reservations. This has also created a few challenges in terms of pricing on these sites compared to the hotel's site, and the adverse effect on profitability from discounted rates on these sites. If used properly, these sites can be an effective tool in managing occupancy and room rates, but like most operators, we prefer to have our guests use our proprietary sites.

Another change in the industry over the past five to ten years is the emphasis on health and fitness. A good fitness facility is now a requirement for many travelers. A spa is an added attraction, and with the current emphasis on healthy eating and low-carb diets, we need to be much more creative in designing menus for our restaurants and banquet facilities.

Both the lodging companies and franchisees have gone from a single brand to multiple brands. Years ago, a Hilton was a Hilton and a Holiday Inn was a Holiday Inn. Today, each of these companies has a wide variety of brands serving a wide variety of customers. Today's franchisees may also operate different brands from different franchisors in different locations.

Lodging companies have also moved from owning and managing their properties to franchising their brand to other owners. They can grow the brand much faster this way, because they can add new locations without the financial impact of owning the real estate.

Looking ahead, I think we will see continued increases in Internet bookings and more electronics in guest rooms. I also believe we will see continued growth in hotels and resorts with water parks, which appeal to busy families seeking a short vacation getaway. Condominium hotels are also growing in popularity. This concept is attractive to people who want to invest in a property they can enjoy themselves, while also benefiting from the potential rental income.

The industry will continue to change, and if you want to thrive on change, you must keep abreast—or, even better, ahead—of changing customer tastes and preferences. We are always looking at trends and what is new in the industry. This is not a static business—it is changing continually, and to be a leader, you must stay ahead of the curve.

To stay on top of the industry, I read continuously. I travel. I attend industry meetings and talk with other chief executive officers—not just in the lodging business, but from all types of businesses. We are always gauging the market and what our guests like and don't like.

Keys to Success

The best advice I ever received was, "Take care of your associates and they will take care of your customers. If you don't take care of your customers, someone else will." I can't emphasize enough how important our people are. This is a people business. We need the best people up and down the line. We want to treat them right and train them right.

Another critical key to success is taking care of the assets. Hotels get a tremendous amount of wear and tear from the public. We are committed to continually reinvesting in our assets—in good times and not-so-good times—to maintain and enhance them. If we wait to replace some carpeting until it looks like it needs to be replaced, it's too late. However, we don't want to do it too early because that wastes money. It's a delicate balance.

In summary, to be successful you need good real estate, a strong balance sheet, an exceptional guest experience, and well-trained associates who love what they do.

Stephen H. Marcus is chairman and chief executive officer of the Marcus Corporation, a Milwaukee-based New York Stock Exchange–listed company that operates in the lodging and entertainment industries. Mr. Marcus joined the company in 1962, was named president and chief operating officer in 1980, became chief executive officer in 1988, and was elected chairman in 1991. Under his leadership, the company has achieved successful growth through a commitment to quality, service, and value.

Active in the lodging industry, Mr. Marcus is a past chairman of the Preferred Hotels Association, and a past president of both the Greater Milwaukee Hotel and Motel Association and the Wisconsin Innkeepers Association.

Success in the Leisure Business

Stephen Bartolin
President, Chief Executive Officer, and Chairman
The Broadmoor

The leisure business is the business of taking care of people and creating memories. There are a number of things that go into creating a successful business in the industry. First, reputation and guest loyalty is befitting. On the business side, it is just as important to create value in the asset by generating cash flow and growing the business each year as it is to create value in the asset of the owner.

Second, all involved in the leisure business have pride in what they do. The ownership has pride, and the staff has pride, and the guests have pride in being part of the place. If you put all of those ingredients together, you would have a pretty successful business. We are truly an independent hotel. We are not affiliated with any brand or chain. We are a privately owned versus a publicly traded company. It is a great advantage, because ownership can look at decision making more on a long-term basis. That's a contrast from public companies that are beholden to whatever analyst report comes out that quarter and making knee-jerk decisions accordingly. A lot of hotels that are part of publicly traded companies have to deal with that as a way of life. We can look more long term in our decision making. That is a real plus. The real test to measure success is the test of time. Instead of doing something really well for a few years, doing something well for twenty to twenty-five years is the real measure of success.

Selling the Experience

The experience is everything. In a destination resort, that is exactly what we are selling. We are not selling a guestroom for someone who is passing through town and has meetings elsewhere during the day. We are a destination unto ourselves. The experience is a multitude of things. It is how the guests are greeted when they first pull into our front entrance, how the staff uses their name and how they are greeted in every guest quarter, lobby, and as they walk around the lake.

We are a hotel with history. We opened our doors in June of 1918, so it has character in its architecture. It's in one of the most magnificent settings you could ever have for a resort. It has continuity, which doesn't sound like a lot, but it means so much to our guests and our employees. We have had only two owners since 1918. Our chef is the fourth executive chef since

1918. When you look at the way hotels are owned today, they are bought and sold by some kind of institutional ownership and are an asset on the balance sheet. In our case, there is more of an emotional attachment to that relationship, and that comes through in what kind of place this is to work and how the guests experience it.

We compete in a world where the best is just good enough. Everything we offer in terms of an experience, whether it is dining or going to the outdoor pool, whether it is the spa or golf, has to be the best of the best. We try to deliver on that expectation level. Woven through all those quality experiences are the interactions in between with our staff in making it personal, making it friendly, and making it warm. If you put all that together when you have first-class amenities and facilities, a beautiful environment, and you surround that with warmth and genuine friendliness and personalization from the staff, that is an experience that means something to the guests.

Awards and Honors

There are two top ratings a hotel can get: the Mobile Five Star Award and the AAA Five Diamond Award. We have won the Mobil Five Star Award for forty-four consecutive years. The closest runner-up is the Ritz Carlton in Naples and the Inn at Little Washington. Both of those are at sixteen years. If you look at the number of not just resorts but hotels and lodging establishments of any kind on the North American continent, there are only twelve properties that have Mobil Five Stars and AAA Five Diamonds next to them. The Broadmoor is just a special place in America.

Sustaining Profitability

There are two theories about profitability in this business. Some people feel that if you deliver the ultimate in service, the financials automatically follow. But some people are really good on delivering the service level, but don't know how to get to the bottom line. The other side is the people who are good about knowing how to get to the bottom line, but don't know how to do the service part. The real art form in the business is knowing how to do both successfully. Providing world-class facilities and services, you have to generate a sufficient amount of cash flow, and you have to be able to grow that every year. Just as important, you have to create value in the asset, and if you do all of these things, you will be successful.

We are able to sustain profitability largely from the commitment to be in this business for the long term versus the short term. We are able to reinvest at a higher level in our property. We are always doing something new, something creative, staying abreast and ahead of the marketplace, giving guests a reason to come back. We are doing something every year to make people want to come back. That is probably the most significant way to ensure growth and profitability.

In terms of the most profitable offerings, most hotels are weighted heavily on the room side of the business and they will do some food and beverage. In our resort, only 43 percent of the revenue comes off rooms. There are so many other things people spend money on. Rooms are certainly the most profitable thing any hotel does. The margin on selling a guest room is much higher than any other aspect of the business. The other things—such as food and beverage, golf, spa, tennis, retail, and private club membership—all have a lot of synergy and intertwine.

Setting Rates

Generally, the market tells you where your rates are going to be. A lot of that has to do with marrying the rate with what you are offering. You study your competition and what the market is paying. You listen to your customers, and somewhere in the middle of all that, you come up with your rates. There is no true science to it, but the market will dictate. Like in any real estate asset, the market runs in cycles. We saw enormous rate growth from 1995 to 2000 as most of the industry did. In the last few years, we have been doing better than most since September 11 and since the economy tumbled. We have been able to sustain our rate, and we are actually seeing some pretty good rate growth this year. In 2001, 2002, and 2003, our rates were flat, so you run through those cycles, too. We were able to sustain our occupancy through that, so we came out pretty good, but you go through those cycles in the course of the business.

Seasonality in a resort is always a factor in rates. May through October is our peak time when we are generating our peak rates. Those rates come down in November and December. They will start back up in March and April, and then back to the season. That is pretty common.

Largest Expenses

In any hotel, resort, or city hotel, your largest expense is always labor. The big expense outside of that are capital expenditures, which is different than an operating expense. The investment back in the property is powerful in the resorts, especially when you have an older property. It takes a real commitment on ownership's part for continued capital improvements.

Developing Loyalty

In terms of loyalty, we have an advantage because we have been here a long time. We are a singular property. Some people may find it hard to compete against all the branded properties out there today, but in some ways it even gives us an advantage because we are unique and have our style and our own personality. Guests respond to that, and that helps build loyalty. We also have the advantage of history, because so many guests who have come here have been introduced to us by their parents or grandparents. That is a plus as well.

Measuring Customer Service

The guests are the most honest critics. If you listen carefully to them, they will let you know how the customer service is. Every hotel has guest comment forms, but ours are a little unique in that they don't have a checklist. Our forms thank the guests for being with us and ask for their candid feedback about their experience here. It gives them a place to write on the front and back, and they will tell you so much more that way. Every one is personally responded to, and then we track these and break out all the comments by category, and we monitor them month to month and year to year as a measurement tool. The best way you can tell that you are providing excellent customer service is by the guests letting you know.

Obviously, if you are an experienced hotelier, you have a good sense of how you are delivering, but mostly your customers tell you.

Marketing the Resort

We do our share of consumer advertising. On the group side, it is much more targeted. We do that directly with the groups, and we do that through all the trade publications and incentive houses. Consumer advertising is done through newspapers, direct mail, e-mail, and various high-end consumer and travel publications.

Hiring and Training Staff

One of the qualities to look for in a staff and management team is attitude. We select people on attitude first and experience second. We find that to be a winning formula. We have the most comprehensive, well-defined training development program of any independent hotel in America. We will teach you the business and help you along, but you can't teach attitude. Attitude is number one.

Our training program is unique from others in its scope and in our financial commitment. For an independent hotel, we have five training managers. We have over eighty-six programs offering different training sections that people go through, starting with new hires and refining it by division in food and beverage or rooms division or housekeeping. It breaks out into those specific areas. We have ongoing supervisory training, and management training programs for our management staff. You are only going to be as successful as your staff allows you to be. You are successful only if you surround yourself with quality people.

To prepare for a career in the industry, you can go to a business school or to a college that specializes in hospitality or hotel training, like Cornell or Michigan State. The biggest thing in addition to that is just working in the field. Having a business degree or marketing degree or a degree specifically in hotel management, and combining that degree with an effort to actually work in the field during college, tells a whole lot.

A Culture of Fun

We are all pretty much in this for the long haul. Our executive committee and all of us have made a career commitment to this place because it is such a unique environment and the ownership is so special and the quality of life here is great. It is unique in the American hotel business today. We are fortunate to be part of that. People who are professionals and have experience working with other companies quickly see that. We have a culture where we have fun. We have a culture where we appreciate and respect one another. Each and every person who is part of this organization feels they are treated with dignity and respect. No one is any better than anyone else. If we treat each other that way, it is going to rub off on how our guests experience their time with us.

Choosing a Location

If you are building or buying a destination resort, you look for certain elements in choosing a location. Obviously, the more convenient access you can have with good air service, the better. If you have a good drive market within a five-hundred radius, and a huge population hub in that radius, that is a plus. Those are some demographics that work, but most of all in a destination resort, you have to have magic in the location where it sits. It has to be breathtaking in terms of how it sits on the property.

If an opportunity came to us to buy a property that we felt had a magical setting with some history and some character to the architecture, but perhaps time had not been kind to it but you could bring it back to life with the right investment, that is the kind of thing we would be looking at for an additional investment.

Biggest Challenges and Misconceptions

The challenges in the industry are ongoing. It is kind of a race without a finish line. You always have new competition coming up with fresh ideas and giving people more choices at which to vacation or hold business conferences. The whole industry has had challenges for staffing their hotels with quality people and coming up with creative solutions for that. Day in and day out, the biggest challenge is being consistent with the delivery of service. That is the hardest thing.

Some of the misconceptions of the business—especially on the resort side—are that this is just a lot of fun and recreation and pampered lifestyle. People don't see beneath that veneer to know that there is a lot of hard work that goes into making it this way. That is probably the biggest misconception. A lot of people who really have not worked in the field before get into it and are shocked at what is required of them. It is a twenty-four hours a day, seven days a week, 365 days a year business. When other businesses are on holiday, that is when we are at our busiest. The commitments on weekends are no exception. Those are our busiest times in the resort industry. A lot of people who are getting into the business a little later in life are a bit shocked at understanding the commitments it takes to be successful.

Keeping Your Edge

I have been around the business for almost thirty years, and I am involved in national associations and state associations. There are committees like the American Hotel Lodging Association's resort committee where once a year the operators of most of the top resorts in America get together for four days and there are educational meetings, speakers, and seminars. Largely, however, it is four days of breakfast, lunch, and dinner with my peers. There are other industry organizations like that. Through all those meetings, you are constantly talking to the top operators of the business. We exchange ideas and information, and that is probably the biggest source.

As the chief executive officer, I make sure I am responding to the needs of ownership and delivering what they want out of this business. Managing up is important in any organization, but we are lucky in that our ownership and I really think alike, and their love for this place is real. Their commitment is long term and they are really nice people. I like them and I respect them, so that means quite a lot in terms of being able to do a better job. That ownership relationship continues and always will be important. Beyond that, it is keeping your throttle right to the floorboard at all times and staying on top of every detail. I always think of the big picture, but I get involved in even the smallest details. If you try to manage these things in a more absentee way and be successful at the level we operate at, you are kidding yourself.

Planning for the Future

If you plan on being around, you better be able to look to the future. I don't believe much in ten-year plans. They don't mean a whole lot, because there are market dynamics and economic dynamics that nobody can anticipate. You better be looking out at least three years, and on major issues five years, and have a pretty good idea of where you are going.

I see my job not only as a manager or a chief executive officer of a company. It is just as much a stewardship. The Broadmoor is a national treasure. That is the way I look at it and try to lead it. If I accomplish anything, it is to hand it down in pristine condition both physically and financially for the next generation of employees and guests. Everything I do is toward that goal.

In order to preserve the business physically, you do it with a lot of TLC. It is not just putting money into it—it is putting money into it in the right places and doing it sensitively. Respect for the history of the hotel is important. Everything we do, we do for the future, but we do it with a careful eye on the past. We study the original landscape plans to make sure that what we are doing is keeping with the original thought. There is a real careful eye on history and architectural continuity, as well as preservation and not just building something new.

The Right Time to Expand

In order to stay competitive and be able to compete among the best, you need to expand and grow. We are in the midst of building a new 60,000-square-foot convention center. We are also building a residential community on some land across from the main entrance of the hotel that was used for a variety of commercial purposes over the decades. We tore all those unattractive commercial businesses down. We are building a 1,000-car underground parking garage so we can clean up all the surface parking and create more green space and more beauty. We are building 160 residential units. These are all projects that are in progress as we speak.

Changes in the Industry

Over the last decade or so, the industry has changed a great deal from the consumer's side. First of all, from 1995 to 2000 there was a seller's market. That cycle is reversed now. For the last four years, it has been more of a buyer's market, both on the consumer and the group side. On the group side, it has changed dramatically in how meetings are scheduled and booked. It used to be that for any kind of significant meeting of 1,000 room nights or more, that meeting would be scheduled at least three years out, sometimes five or eight or ten years out. Now, these meetings are booked so little in advance it is shocking. It is not uncommon for those to be booked three months out now. It is much harder to plan your year because of that phenomenon.

Also, there has been a real shift toward who the purchasers of meetings are. There are a lot of third parties or intermediaries involved in the buying of meetings that act on behalf of companies or organizations that schedule. The buyer is different, and it is a more moving target. There have been some real sea changes on the meeting side.

The Future

I hope that over the last half of this decade, the market improves, because that is always a lot more fun. If the economy continues to improve, you will see more and more meetings scheduled. Certainly, we will see more leisure purchasing via the Web. Other than that, I don't see any real dramatic shifts over the next three to four years.

In order to thrive in the changing marketplace, you need to understand it, be aware of it, and keep up with it. It is fast-paced, and you better have a staff that has the marketing savvy to know how to do that—especially in an independent hotel. We don't have a multiple-hotel brand out there with lots of national advertising.

Best Piece of Advice

The best piece of advice would be to take care of the little things, and the big things will tend to take care of themselves.

Stephen Bartolin is a graduate of Youngstown State University in Youngstown, Ohio, with a B.S. degree in business. He joined the Greenbrier in 1975, where he held management positions in the golf operations, front office, reservations, food and beverage, conference services, and sales.

In 1980, Mr. Bartolin left the Greenbrier to become director of convention services at Opryland Hotel in Nashville, Tennessee, a position he held for five years. In 1985, he was promoted to resident manager at Opryland Hotel, which at the time was a 1,100-room facility with 225,000 square feet of meeting and convention space.

In September of 1987, Mr. Bartolin returned to the Greenbrier as general manager at the 6,500-acre, 650-room destination resort.

In July of 1991, Mr. Bartolin became president of the Broadmoor in Colorado Springs, Colorado. Since then, the Broadmoor has added 150 rooms (700 total), a new golf club, a world-class spa facility, a new pool complex, lakeside suites, a $35 million restoration of the original main building, and refurbishment of the entire hotel, grounds, and golf courses. Progress continues with the addition of the 60,000 square foot Broadmoor Hall, the addition of a new restaurant, eight new retail shops, and a rebuild of the 144-room south building. In 1999, Mr. Bartolin was made chief executive officer, and in 2002 he was named chairman. He also serves as chairman, president, and chief executive officer of the Manitou & Pikes Peak Railway Company, the Cog Land and Development Company, and the Broadmoor Golf Club. Mr. Bartolin is on the board of the Broadmoor's parent company, the Oklahoma Publishing Company.

Mr. Bartolin was named 1997 Resort Executive of the Year.

Cushioning Your Profits

Robert B. Trussell Jr.
Chief Executive Officer
Tempur-Pedic International

Consumer Products Leadership Strategies

As the Baby Boomer population ages, the trend for high-end, differentiated consumer products will be that products that offer a value-added proposition and can separate themselves in some way from the rest can be sold at a premium. Basically, in our business, products can become less commoditized as they set themselves apart.

In the mattress industry, we are decommoditizing mattresses. Traditionally, mattresses have been a commodity, meaning that consumers had no brand allegiance with very few people knowing on what brand they were sleeping. We're changing that. People have made the same type of changes in other categories or product spectrums in which products have become popular and known to be superior to what's out there. When that happens, the money ceases to become the reason why consumers buy something. Cost becomes less important and, therefore, you can drive the business with higher margins, which allows you to build your brand with marketing dollars as you reinvest.

What Sets Us Apart

The difference in our company is that we provide products that are performance-based in an industry that has traditionally been sold on looks. Mattresses have fancy ticking on the outside, and the more expensive ones are even thicker, plusher, and better looking. We didn't really think that made much sense, especially with a product hidden in the consumers' bedrooms covered with sheets. Our intention was to come up with a product that truly benefited the consumer. We employed the technology of a product that actually was used in hospitals and nursing homes where mattress performance is critical—if it doesn't work, patients get bedsores.

We developed the new technology and first introduced it through the medical sector, starting with hospitals and nursing homes. Then, we tackled specific problems, such as back pain, by targeting a network of worldwide chiropractors. At that point, we realized that the reason these mattresses perform in a clinical study was the same thing that made them more comfortable: they were pressure-relieving products. We took functional products and brought them to the consumer side. Even though our product might not look as good as the traditional inner springs, we were able to sell this as a value-added proposition. We are changing the industry.

Generating Growing Revenues and Profits

As a startup company in 1992, Tempur-Pedic is still relatively small and still only 5 or 6 percent of the worldwide mattress market, which is a big industry. We achieve our growth by grabbing market share. We do concentrate on the premium end of the market, which does narrow our focus slightly, although our value-added proposition allows us to pull consumers up who would never normally consider buying a $1,000 or $1,500 mattress. The proposition intrigues people who might be pulled beyond the original $600 or $700 mattress because of the value-added proposition. Our mattresses are temperature-sensitive and soften when your body comes in contact. This causes it to be a body-friendly, pressure-relieving surface that translates to better comfort, less tossing and turning, and therefore a better night's sleep.

To achieve growth, we continually advertise to increase brand awareness, which started out at zero and is now still quite a bit less than our innerspring competition. Our massive advertising campaign will improve that. Basically, we reinvest in the business in the form of our advertising to build brand awareness and achieve growth. At the same time, we are increasing our distribution base, which started out at zero as well. We've found that as consumers and retailers start to know our brand better, they become more receptive to our products.

Opening new markets, which we continually do, is another way to achieve growth. We're in more than sixty countries now, making us the only truly global brand in mattresses. We are under-penetrated in a lot of areas, so we're trying to open up those markets. For the most part, the plan is the same everywhere—increasing brand awareness and distribution points.

Biggest Challenges

The most challenging part of the business has always been keeping up with the growth. As soon as we build a factory, it seems as if it's at maximum capacity and we have to build another one. The same goes for our infrastructure—our warehousing, our office facilities. Personnel issues also pose a challenge, since you always feel that you have one or two people less than you ought to in a given area. Overall, our most challenging aspect hasn't been the competition; it's been executing our plan.

The other challenge is predicting where the plan is going. When you reach a critical mass and an unknown product starts to become known, everyone can be a potential customer. Trying to judge how fast your growth is going to occur is not easy. In fact, especially in the last few years, we have tended to guess on the low side, and that's a high-class problem to have when you sell more than you expect. But that is the biggest challenge.

Deciding on the Right Product Mix

It's important for a company to realize what its business is and to focus on its core business and not to spread out into other peripheral products until the time is right. At one point, we made the mistake of not following this rule. We started getting into chairs, footwear, and other products because this Tempur–Pedic material can be used to make a lot of different things. Exploit your core products or your core business model before venturing out into new areas. Use your market share to judge.

Tempur-Pedic is 5 percent of the mattress market worldwide. When we get up around 25 percent or so, we can say, "Hey, we're probably maximizing what we're going to be here—let's look for a new trick." Before that point, adding to our focus or going down divergent paths would be a distraction to the organization.

Following our traditional "pull" model in which we advertise nationally, instead of a "push" model where we would pay the stores with co-op, commissions, or slotting allowances to get floor space, helps us take market share from our competitors. We create demand, on the other hand, through our advertising to the point where people go to the stores and ask for the product. That is how we get the floor space. When our representative makes his or her call, the store owner will say, "Well yeah, let's talk because I had ten people come in here in the last two weeks and ask about your products."

So that's what drives our business—creating demand through our advertising model. We use the direct-response advertising model with the 800 number—call for a free video is the message we try to get across. We don't encourage customers to go to the stores, because we want to sell direct over the phone if possible. What that does is create awareness that mattresses are a destination shopping event.

When people come into the market for a mattress—they just realized they need a new mattress or they have a back problem or something—they think of us because we are trying to be everywhere as far as media goes. We're on television, on the radio, in newspapers, and in magazines, so wherever consumers look they're likely to see us or hear about us, which helps them think of us during the eventual buying decision.

Our goal is to be in everybody's zone of consideration. We realize that not everybody will buy our mattress or our pillows, but we know that if people are aware of our products, we'll sell quite a few. If people are not aware of our products, we won't sell much, so we try to make people aware. Years ago in the mattress industry, when the waterbed craze got to be about 10 to 15 percent of the overall mattress market, people were starting to think, "Well, should we get a waterbed this time, honey?" Waterbeds were in the zone of consideration. This example is a little different, because waterbeds were truly a fad and the source of problems with few real benefits. Our goal is to get in that zone—but instead of a waterbed, we have a product that is a real breakthrough in sleep surface technology.

Profit Percentages

We have different channels, so generalizing our profit percentages is difficult because we sell both direct to the consumer and, wholesale to stores. We try to develop a business model that gives us sufficient margins to make us profitable and to have the money to reinvest in the business in the form of infrastructure and advertising. The different channels have different margins. As a company, we have a gross profit margin of about 52 percent and operating margins of about 22 percent.

Staying Ahead of the Curve

We try to improve our products constantly. Years ago, our mattress covers and pillows were inferior to what we offer now. We're always trying to improve the products themselves and the packaging because they do tend to get stale, especially in retail environments, and to come out with new products. For many years, all we had was one basic mattress model. It came in different sizes, but it was the same model. Now, we've got three and we'll come out with one new model or so per year, so three years from now we'll have six mattresses. On the pillow front, we have about nine pillow sizes and shapes. That's the way we do it—we freshen up with new products and improve existing products.

The first golden rule for success in this industry would be to offer functional products. The second is to build brand awareness. The third is to focus on the premium sector of the market.

Reducing Corporate Spending

Creating a strategy to help reduce corporate spending is a challenge. We have been in a mode of increasing corporate spending because of going public and Sarbanes-Oxley. Our director and officer insurance, for example, increased more than tenfold when we became a public company. So getting a grip on that is difficult, because these are all under the topic of things we have to do. When you have to do something, you can't say, "Let's not do it, let's put it off," because you've got auditors, lawyers, financial people, and banks saying you've got to do it. We're in a period of high corporate spending—way more than anything we could have budgeted for—and after the dust settles and we pass the Sarbanes-Oxley test, we can stabilize that spending. So, that's a big problem, trying to manage your corporate budget. Any other budget in the company—sales, marketing, information technology, whatever—you have options. With corporate budgets in this regulatory environment, options are limited. Going forward, certainly, we will try to make the corporate budget just as accountable as any other budget. Right now, it's tough.

Ultimately, we'll be able to trim legal expenses by bringing a lawyer in-house. The same applies with some of the audit issues—we can bring consultants in-house, which will reduce the need for the consultants and bring the cost down. Just focusing on corporate spending will bring ways to reduce it. The key is to treat it like a traditional budget rather than a have-to-do budget.

Common Areas of Overspending

One mistake is trying to become a retailer, which can be very expensive. That decision is risky, and the business model is expensive and problematic. Although many succeed, for every one that does, ten don't. Choosing your business model is critical, because that dictates where you spend your money.

For some departments, companies can reduce costs by following general guidelines. For us, for example, keeping marketing costs in check is all about negotiating advertising, which could mean better deals with media buyers or media, magazines, newspapers, radio, and so on.

When it comes to information technology, managers should be focusing more on what we really need than what we can do. Information technology tends to get caught up in the bells and whistles and, "having this or that would be cool."

In the area of operations, personnel issues, and making the various departments and administration more efficient, are the best ways to reduce costs. We try to staff better people, even if we have fewer of them. Automation is certainly another way to reduce costs.

For manufacturing, continuously improving manufacturing efficiencies will reduce expenses.

Overall, we are a growth business, growing 25 to 50 percent a year, so cost cutting is not as big a focus for us as it is in other companies. Companies growing at a much slower rate, for example, have to rely on efficiencies and cost cutting to maintain profitability. Our focus has been on growth. Of course, we try to run things as efficiently as possible, but we do not prioritize that. We prioritize growing another 50 percent, not how few people we could use for something. We're always hiring. We've never laid people off.

Robert B. Trussell Jr. is the chief executive officer of Tempur-Pedic International and a member of Tempur-Pedic International's board of directors. He has served in these capacities at Tempur-Pedic International or its predecessor since 2000. From 1992 to 2000, Mr. Trussell served as president of Tempur-Pedic Inc., one of the predecessors to Tempur-Pedic International.

Prior to joining Tempur-Pedic International, Mr. Trussell was general partner of several racing limited partnerships that owned racehorses in England, France, and the United States. He was also the owner of several startup businesses in the equine lending and insurance business.

Mr. Trussell received his B.S. degree from Marquette University.

C-LEVEL BUSINESS INTELLIGENCE · C-LEVEL BUSINESS INTELLIGENCE ·
ASPATORE BOOKS